British Parachute Fo 194

by Howard P.Davies
Series Editor Brian L.Davis

Published by
Arco Publishing Company, Inc.,
219 Park Avenue South,
New York, N.Y. 10003.

Library of Congress Catalog
Card Number 73-83741
ISBN 0—668—03362—2

Printed in Great Britain.
Series Editor: Brian L. Davis, for
Key Military Publications
Series Design: David Gibbons, for
Arms and Armour Press

Typesetting: ABCDesign
Camerawork: Duotech Graphics
Limited
Printed in England

Acknowledgements
The author acknowledges with
thanks the invaluable assistance
given by Brian L. Davis in the
preparation of this book; and
Colour Sergeant T. Fitch, Curator
of the Museum of the Parachute
Regiment and Airborne Forces
Aldershot, for help in establishing and verifying several
details. Photographs reproduced
are from the collection of the
Imperial War Museum, London,
and the Bundesarchiv, Koblenz
(plate 4).

Contents

Plate 1. *Newly air-dropped paratroopers bring their parachute canopies under control. This photo clearly shows the vent (the circular hole) in the canopy of the parachute. The British 'X' type statichute was generally regarded as of a much superior design to any other type of parachute in use during the Second World War. The harness with which this type of parachute was equipped was of considerably better design than that used by the German parachute forces. During an airborne descent the soldier was able to exercise a fair degree of control over his parachute by pulling on the lift webs. The weight of his body was disposed evenly in the harness, thus sparing him the extensive body bruises to which the German paratrooper was subjected. He was given sufficient freedom of movement to allow him to take the shock on landing with feet and knees placed tightly together. Gradual development of the parachute also ensured less body shock and discomfort. A quick-release box fitted to the harness made it possible for the soldier to get out of the parachute within a few seconds of landing.*

Historical Background

When Great Britain declared war on Germany on 3rd September 1939 airborne troops did not rank amongst her fighting forces. The existence of German parachute units had been known to the British long before the outbreak of war, but it was the overwhelming successes the Germans achieved with the use of parachute and glider-borne troops in their assaults on the Belgian forts of Eben-Emal, on Narvik in Norway and Rotterdam in the Netherlands that finally dispelled any doubts that may have existed in the minds of the British war leaders as to whether this type of formation was of any practical use or not.

A memo by the wartime Prime Minister, Winston Churchill, in June 1940 stated: 'We ought to have a Corps of at least 5,000 parachute troops . . . ' It was addressed to the head of the Military Wing of the War Cabinet Secretariat, General Ismay, who received it on 22nd June 1940. At about the same time it had already been decided to establish an Airborne Forces training centre at Ringway, near Manchester. This was named the 'Central Landing School' under the joint jurisdiction of the Royal Air Force and the Army, with Major J.F.Rock, Royal Engineers, in charge of the military organisation of British airborne forces.

They had six Whitley aircraft (plate 5) and very little else. In July 1940 the first practice jumps were made from the Whitley bombers, which had each been fitted with a small platform in place of the rear turret. The parachute was opened with the man still on the platform, and he was thereafter literally pulled off the aircraft into the air. Men of No.2 Commando were selected for training in parachute duties, and with no previous experience in this form of training the British Command had to rely on ideas gleaned from the German airborne forces. This German influence was very evident, especially in some of the earlier equipment and clothing worn by the British parachute troops. (See plates 3, 4.)

The title of No.2 Commando was changed first to No.11 Special Air Service Battalion, then to the 1st Parachute Battalion. In September 1941 the 1st Parachute Battalion was joined by formations of volunteers, which had been raised in August 1941, with the title of the 2nd and 3rd Parachute Battalions.

The techniques of parachute operations were gradually improved, and all through the summer and early autumn of 1940 rigorous training went on. It was the task of the RAF to produce the parachute equipment, to evolve the methods of dropping and to teach the troops their air technique. (See plates 6-13.) Meanwhile the Army studied the special organisation for fighting on the ground and the weapons and tactical training of the parachutists (plates 67, 68, 69, 71, 72). Shortly after Christmas 1940 a sufficient number of troops had been trained to a high enough pitch to make a small-scale operation possible.

In August 1940 the establishment at Ringway was re-named the 'Central Landing Establishment'. It became the cradle of British Airborne Forces and was commanded at that time by Group Captain L.G.Harvey (plate 14).

The attack on the Tragino aqueduct, near Monte Voltore in Southern Italy (1,800 miles from Britain), the first British airborne operation of the Second World War, was carried out by a volunteer force consisting of 38 men commanded by Major T.A. Pritchard, Royal Welch Fusiliers. This force, using the island of Malta as its base, dropped from Whitley bombers of 91 Squadron Royal Air Force during the early hours of 11th February 1941. The force succeeded in carrying home their attack on the aqueduct but, despite the demolition of a section of the superstructure, once the destruction was discovered the Italians were able to repair the damage before any appreciable effects were felt on the towns which the aqueduct supplied. The overall effect on

2. Airborne invasion exercises were at times carried out in England with British and Canadian airborne troops co-operating together with the US Army Air Force Troop Carrier Squadron; the latter, based in the UK, was responsible for supplying air transport for all Allied airborne forces.
This photograph shows British airborne troops making a perfect landing in the 'Battle Area' during one such exercise.

3. Left: *British paratroops assisting each other in adjustments to their equipment before leaving for a practice drop.*

4. Below left: *German paratroopers making adjustments to their equipment before emplaning for a practice drop over a training area. Max Schmelling, the boxer, who was a volunteer in the German parachute arm, is shown in the foreground. The similarity between the German and early British paratroop forces was very marked and is clearly shown in these two photos.*

5. Above right: *Men and supplies parachute from an early RAF Whitley bomber. Dakotas replaced the old Whitleys in 1942.*

6. Centre right: *General Sir John Dill, C. in C. Home Forces, inspecting one of the first batches of trainee paratroops at RAF Ringway, Manchester, in December 1940. The men are wearing a form of close fitting leather flying helmet, one of the first forms of protective headdress used by British parachute forces. The special crepe soled high lace-up boots being worn here were very similar to the German parachute boots. These were eventually discarded in favour of the normal pattern army-issue ankle boots with leather soles and studs. Two men in the front rank are wearing miniature wing and parachute badges above the left pocket of their battledress blouses. The trainees were made up of volunteers, mostly from infantry regiments; however, it will be seen that there is an officer from the Royal Tank Regiment standing just to the side of General Dill.*

7. Right: *Trainee parachutists at Ringway, December 1940, being inspected before boarding the RAF Whitley aircraft used for their practice jumps.*

8. Above left: *Parachute recruits under instruction learning how to land and roll by jumping from an elevated springboard.*

9. Below left: *An RAF Warrant Officer instructor shown wearing the special parachute instructor's badge on his right upper arm. The recruit on the 'mat' is being taught how to turn himself from his harness while being dragged along the ground.*

10. Centre: *Fully trained paratroops on parade at Ringway after completing the training course. The squads are accompanied by their RAF instructors.*

11. Above right: *Paratroops receiving orders just prior to boarding aircraft at Netheravon in 1942.*

12. Below right: *Paratroops at Ringway in 1942 wearing the rimless steel helmets camouflaged with dark green netting covers.*

the enemy was negligible. The whole of the landing force was captured, and one of the accompanying interpreters, Fortuanto Picchi (an Italian who formerly worked at the Savoy Hotel in London), as a result was court-martialled and shot in Rome. This first practical experiment in the employment of British parachute troops, although the outcome was not successful, did however show the extent to which the joint work of the Army and RAF had developed within a few months and it laid the foundation for that co-operation between the two Services which led to such epic events as the leap over the West Wall on D-Day, the Arnhem operation and the Airborne landings on the east bank of the Rhine.

The second operation came about when it was decided to attack the German radar installation at Bruneval, about twelve miles north of Le Havre in northern France. This raid (plates 15, 16) took place on 27th February 1942. The paratroops dropped from bombers led by Wing Commander P.C.Pickard and they were commanded by Major J.C.Frost. This operation proved successful and a good part of the German radar equipment was brought back to England.

In November 1941 Major-General F.A.M.Browning (plate 32) was appointed GOC of the Airborne Forces. It was by the authority of this officer that the 1st Parachute Brigade became known as the Red Devils. The name derived from the distinctive headgear of the paratroops — the maroon beret. The description was reputed to have been used initially by the Germans, and was passed on to Major-General Browning by General Alexander with the inference that the nickname was to be taken as a compliment. The name has remained as the semi-official title for British airborne forces ever since.

13. Above left: *British parachutists dropping from a Whitley aircraft during an airborne demonstration held in the presence of HM the King at Windsor on 25th May 1941.*

14. Above right: *British officers in charge of parachute training, from left to right, Brigadier R.N. Gale, Group Captain L.G. Harvey, Wing Commander M.A. Newnham, Lieutenant-Colonel E.E. Down, CO 1st Parachute Battalion, and Major Hope-Thompson.*

15. Centre right: *Air Marshal Sir Arthur Barratt, Air Officer Commander-in-Chief, Army Co-operation Command (left) and General Sir Bernard Paget (right) talking to paratroops at Ringway, July 1942.*

16. Below right: *Training on the Dorset coast in February 1942 for the raid on the German Radar installation at Bruneval. Note the parachutists' fighting knives and helmets.*

By the end of 1942, Dakota aircraft were being used for 'drops' (plate 17) providing some considerable improvement on the Whitley bombers.

The 1st Parachute Brigade provided the nucleus of the 1st Airborne Division, which first saw action in French North Africa (November 1942) in an engagement known as 'Operation Torch'. The 1st Parachute Brigade, in support of the British 1st Army landings, secured and captured the airfield at Bône. A further airborne force landed at Souk el Araba airfield east of Algiers and there was much confused fighting before the two forces linked up with the 1st Army. At the onset of winter (1942-43) the 1st Parachute Brigade fought with distinction as infantry. In the meantime the 6th Airborne Division was formed in May 1943 under the command of Major-General R.N.Gale (plate 33). The troops comprised men from the 3rd Parachute Brigade, 5th Parachute Brigade, 6th Air Landing Brigade and a Canadian Parachute Battalion.

After the action in North Africa the 1st Airborne Division prepared for the invasion of Sicily in July 1943. Glider-borne troops landed on the island on 9th/10th July, and the paratroops landed three days later in the region of Syracuse. The 1st Airborne Division also took part in the invasion of the Italian mainland, capturing Castellaneta and Foggia before being relieved and returning to England at the end of 1943.

Meanwhile the 6th Airborne Division was undergoing the most strenuous training and preparation, for it was destined to play a very important part in the invasion of Europe (plates 18, 19, 20, 21). Its task would be to protect the flank of the D-Day assault of 6th June 1944, to the left of 'Sword' beach north-east of the town of Caen. After being involved in extremely heavy fighting around Caen the division became continuously engaged for over eight weeks. From 17th August 1944 the 6th Airborne advanced steadily eastwards until it reached Honfleur. It was a seriously depleted formation that returned home to England to rest and re-organise a few months later.

In December the Division was again in action, fighting in the western tip of the Ardennes salient under the command of Major-General E.Bols (plate 34), who at that time was one of the youngest generals in the British Army. The 6th Airborne again returned to the United Kingdom in the New Year—1945—to prepare for its next operation.

For the 1st Airborne Division the next action was Arnhem. Their part in the attempt to end the war in Europe by the winter of 1944-45 won them undying fame. The objective was the seizure by airborne assault of the three bridges in the Netherlands over the rivers Maas and Rhine (at Grave, Nijmegen and Arnhem), which would facilitate a drive to the east, outflanking German forces in the Ruhr. The road bridge at Nijmegen was taken intact by British troops on 20th September 1944, while 1st Airborne fought gallantly and desperately from 17th to 25th September. But their efforts were in vain: their objective was not achieved and the bridge remained firmly in the hands of the Germans. Of the 10,000 men who landed in the Arnhem area, fewer than 3,000 came back across the Rhine for withdrawal to England.

The Battle for Arnhem (plates 23-26) was a vicious slogging match for the troops on both sides. There was no let-up throughout the whole period. Because they were slowly being squeezed into a smaller area by overwhelming German forces, supplies which the British troops so badly needed were air-dropped out of their reach into the German lines. The German units in opposition to the British were hard fighters, veterans of the campaigns in Russia, and included amongst them the 9.SS-Panzer-Division

17. Top left: *RAF Dakotas from 46 Group Transport Comn and air drop supplies. The men and machines from this group spearheaded all three major airborne operations in Europe—Normandy, Arnhem and the Rhine. Their D-Day task was to drop 2,300 paratroops and 1,000 gliderborne troops. They carried men, food, supplies and ammunition to the forward battle areas and brought back the wounded.*
18. Top right: *As part of the preparation for the invasion of Europe, soldiers of the 6th Airborne Division are seen here at pay parade, when they received French invasion currency.*
19. Centre left: *Pathfinders of 6th Airborne Division, who were the first to land in France just prior to the main assault on the coast, are briefed. Their task was to act as guides for the following force of parachutists. Note in photographs 18 and 19 the extra large map pocket on the right leg of the battledress trousers normally worn by airborne troops for operational duties.*
20. Centre right: *Paratroops boarding a glider en route for the battle just after the initial D-Day landings.*
21. Bottom: *Gliders in a field in Normandy used as a landing area during the invasion of 1944.*

22. Above Left: *Photographers of the Army Film and Photographic Unit who took the Arnhem pictures of 1st Airborne Division. Left to right, Sergeant Smith from Manchester, who was wounded in the right shoulder, Sergeant Walker, a Scot, and Sergeant Lewis, a Londoner.*
The Battle for Arnhem was fought by the 1st Airborne Division from 17th to 25th September 1944. These selected

photos show the British troops in action.
23. Above centre: *Clearing a school-house on the outskirts of Arnhem.*
24. Above right: *A six-pounder anti-tank gun in action.*

25. Below left: *Paratroops in action, dug in with a 3in mortar, 20 September 1944.*
26. Below right: *Troops of the 1st Parachute Battalion in action at Arnhem, on 17th September 1944.*

27: *Officers and men of the Lancashire Parachute Battalion after being decorated at Buckingham Palace on 28th June 1945. At this investiture 114 officers and men of the 6th Airborne Division received decorations from H.M. the King; these included 17 DSOs or bars. The Commanding General, Major-General E.L.Bols, his three brigade commanders, and eight of his nine battalion commanders received DSOs with bars.*

28: *Five men from the 6th Airborne Division after receiving decorations at Buckingham Palace on 28th June 1945.*

29: *Three members of the 6th Airborne Division after the investiture at Buckingham Palace. The centre figure is Lieutenant-Colonel R.G. Pine-Coffin, DSO, MC, Commanding Officer of the Somerset Light Infantry Battalion.*

'Hohenstaufen' and the 10.SS-Panzer-Division 'Frundsberg'. A German war reporter had this to say over the German radio on 27th September about the men of Arnhem: 'They are certainly hardy fellows, the pick of the bunch to whom the British Command entrusted the difficult operations at Arnhem . . . The paratroops had already been driven from the bridge where they landed and held their first positions, but they fought on stubbornly'.

Major-General Urquhart received the insignia of Commander of the Bath from the King at an investiture held at Buckingham Palace on 9th October 1944, and at a another special investiture held by King George VI on 6th December 1944 there were four hundred men of the 'Red Devils' present. The number was unprecedented and, for the first time in history, the ceremony had to be held in the spacious entrance hall of the palace. Sixty-one of the paratroopers received decorations (plates 27, 28, 29) which included one Victoria Cross (Major R.H.Cain, South Staffordshire Regiment), two CBs, seven DSOs, nineteen MCs, seven DCMs and twenty-five MMs. Posthumous VCs were awarded to Captain L.E. Queripel, Lieutenant J.H. Grayburn and Lance-Sergeant J.D. Baskeyfield.

30. Above: *A picture taken on 17th September 1944 at the site of a glider landing area on the outskirts of Arnhem. Note the damaged wing tip which testified to the small landing space available. The jeep and trailer in the foreground belong to the Headquarters Group of Artillery.*

31. Below: *Airborne troops pinned down by heavy German fire beside their crashed glider east of the Rhine on 25th March 1945.*

17

Lieutenant-General Frederick Browning, CB,DSO, received the Order of the Bath at the investiture on 6th December and was appointed to succeed General Sir Henry Pownall as Chief-of-Staff to Lord Louis Mountbatten at South East Asia Command (SEAC) Headquarters on 28th November 1944. Major-General R.N.Gale succeeded Lieutenant-General 'Boy' Browning as deputy commander to the American Lieutenant-General L.H.Brereton of the 1st Allied Airborne Army. The appointment was announced on 18th January 1945.

Field-Marshal Montgomery addressed men of the 6th Airborne Division when he visited troops of the 21st Army Group during their advance from Coesfeld to Osnabrück, which they entered on 3rd April 1945; two days later they reached the river Weser and seized Minden, site of the historic battle in 1759 when British and Hanoverian troops had defeated the French during the Seven Years War.

The operation of crossing the Rhine —the greatest of all airborne operations in the Second World War — was given the code name 'Varsity'. It was to be strictly a joint operation, shared with the American Airborne forces and was to be a glider-borne engagement. The re-equipped 6th British Airborne Division, however, commanded by General Bols along with Major-General M.B.Ridgway commanding the 18th US (Airborne) Corps, was intended merely as a 'bonus' to the land attack across the Rhine. Applying the hard-learnt lessons of Arnhem it was intended that the British landings north of Wesel should be supported from the start by the medium artillery of 21st Army Group. This meant that the British Airborne forces should drop only a mile or two ahead of the land forces, which were intended to effect a junction in a matter of hours, instead of days or weeks. If all went well, overnight a commando brigade would have stormed into Wesel in advance of XXX Corps which was to cross the Rhine on a wide front.

On 24th March 1945 3,000 aircraft carrying some 16,000 airborne troops, both British and American, headed across the Rhine from twenty-six British and Continental bases — the whole formation stretching 75 miles from van to tail. Despite the extremely heavy strafing carried out by rocket firing RAF Typhoons of the area earmarked as the 'dropping zone' for the gliders, so many German flak and machine-gun emplacements survived that of the 416 gliders that landed (plates 30, 31) only 88 were undamaged. Battle casualties in the 6th Airborne Division on the first day totalled 108 officers and 1,300 men killed, wounded and missing — and although some of the missing subsequently turned up the price was high. A bridgehead was, however, established across the Rhine and the airborne forces succeeded in crossing the river Issel, seizing the important railway running from Weel to Bocholt.

The 6th Airborne Division then took part in the advance across Germany, finally reaching the Baltic Sea. Troops of the 6th Airborne linked up with a Russian armoured squadron at Wismar, due north of Schwerin on the bay of Lübeck, on 2nd May, six days before the unconditional surrender of Germany. The 6th Airborne remained in Germany until November 1945 when it was sent to Palestine following riots there.

Royal Air Force Transport Command had meanwhile ferried veterans of Arnhem to Oslo's Gardemoen airfield; they arrived on 11th May 1945 to carry out their last major assignment of the Second World War, and on 15th May Crown Prince Olaf of Norway arrived from the United Kingdom (in a British destroyer) to be welcomed at the quayside by Major-General Urquhart — commanding the 1st Airborne Division.

32. Above left: *Major-General F.A.M. Browning.*
33. Below: *Major-General R.N. Gale.*

34. Above Centre: *Major-General E.L. Bols.*
35. Above right: *Major-General R.E. Urquhart.*

Composition of the British Airborne Forces from 1st September 1944 to 7th May 1945: European Theatre of Operations

The 1st Airborne Division:[1]

Commanding Officer: Major-General R.E.Urquhart.

1st Parachute Brigade: 1st, 2nd and 3rd Parachute Regiments.

4th Parachute Brigade: 10th, 11th and 156th Parachute Regiments

1st Air Landing Brigade: 1st Border Regiment, 2nd South Staffordshire Regiment and 7th King's Own Scottish Borderers.

Divisional Troops: Royal Artillery: 1st Air Landing Light Regiment; Royal Engineers: 1st Airborne Divisional Engineers; Royal Signals: 1st Airborne Divisional Signals.

The 6th Airborne Division:

Commanding Officer: Major-General R.N.Gale (until 7th December 1944); Major-General E.L.Bols (from 8th December 1944).

3rd Parachute Brigade: 8th Parachute Regiment, 9th Parachute Regiment and 1st Canadian Parachute Battalion.

5th Parachute Brigade: 7th, 12th and 13th Parachute Regiments.

6th Air Landing Brigade: 12th Devonshire Regiment, 2nd Oxfordshire and Buckinghamshire Light Infantry, and 1st Royal Ulster Rifles.

Divisional Troops: Royal Armoured Corps: 6th Airborne Armoured Reconnaissance Regiment; Royal Artillery: 53rd Air Landing Light Regiment and 2nd Air Landing Anti-Tank Regiment; Royal Engineers: 6th Airborne Divisional Engineers; Royal Signals: 6th Airborne Divisional Signals.

---

[1] 1st Airborne Division left the European theatre before 7th May 1945.

Uniforms

The uniforms and clothing worn by British paratroops during the Second World War can be divided into two groups:
1. The standard British Army battledress with its various items of canvas web equipment;
2. The special paratroop clothing and equipment used both for training and practice drops, and later for ground combat.

Paratroop Volunteers' Battledress and Insignia
British paratroops were all volunteers, drawn from almost every regiment and branch of the British Army. On joining the training establishment they wore their own uniform which, in the main, consisted of the universally-issued British Army khaki serge battledress, black leather 'ammunition' ankle boots, web gaiters, web waist belt, and headdress. Any cap badges worn or insignia displayed were those of the wearer's parent unit. On qualifying as fully fledged paratroopers they were presented with the coveted 'red beret' (plate 59) and were further distinguished by wearing airborne insignia and 'wings' (plates 18, 37, 71).

British Airborne Special Parachute Clothing and Equipment
The design and manufacture of the basic items of parachute clothing and equipment adopted by the British airborne forces were in the initial stages based largely on ideas gleaned from the equipment and specialist clothing used by the German airborne troops. A damaged parachute and a Fallschirmjäger steel helmet captured from the Germans were the only models available to the Central Landing School on which they could base the design of similar British equipment. Much hard work, trial and error went into this important field of development. Over a period of time many modifications were made to the basic items of protective headdress, clothing and equipment until eventually they were perfected and became standard issue to all ranks throughout the British airborne forces. British parachute clothing, although seemingly complicated, was simple to wear and designed to give the wearer the maximum warmth in the air and the maximum amount of mobility on the ground.

Parachute Harness and Parachutes
Two commercial firms (normally trade rivals in peacetime) combined their skills, energies and work force to produce for the newly established paratroop arm the first of what was to become many thousands of parachutes and sets of harness. The principle of the statichute — that is, a parachute which opened automatically — was already known, and was rapidly developed into an item as near foolproof as any man-made device could be.

To the parachute harness was attached a bag carried on the back of the soldier (plates 38, 45), within which was another bag divided into two compartments and containing the parachute. Upon leaving the aircraft the outside bag remained attached to the soldier's harness, but the inner one was designed to be pulled violently from it by the static line (which was a 12ft 6in length of webbing). At the other end of the static line was a metal 'D' ring which engaged a hook attached to the end of the strop, a length of webbing with its top end secured to a 'strong point' in the aircraft. The strop had to be long enough to ensure that the parachute would be well below the aircraft before it opened, yet short enough so that the parachute was not caught in the slipstream and twisted round the rear of the aircraft or the tailwheel. In a Dakota the strop was attached to a steel cable running along the inside of the aircraft; the strop attachment was clipped to this cable and moved with the jumpers as they shuffled one by one towards the exit.

36. *The badge of the Army Air Corps, first introduced for wear by all ranks of the Parachute Regiment on 1st August 1942.*

37. *The famous 'winged parachute' badge, first introduced in May 1943. This badge superseded that of the Army Air Corps.*

38. Top left: *Paratroopers ready to board an aircraft. The static line is hanging down at the rear of the parachute pack.*
39. Top right: *Paratroops at Ringway bring their parachutes under control after landing.*
40. Below left: *Men of the 6th Royal Welch Parachute Battalion using special camouflaged parachutes, Ringway, August 1942.*
41. Below right: *A paratrooper gathers up the canopy and shroud lines of his 'chute'.*

On jumping from an aircraft the parachutist fell through the
air from one to one-and-a-half seconds before the strop (which
pulled out the static line in the top half of the inner bag) and then
the line itself (which pulled out the parachute from the bottom
half) became taut. When these two operations had taken place
the canopy of the parachute developed, the headlong fall was
checked and the paratrooper began to float towards the earth.
In fact the soldier approached the ground considerably faster than
he appeared to do; the impact felt on landing was compared with
that experienced by jumping blindfold from a height of six to
eight feet.

The canopy of the parachute was usually made of nylon fabric,
though sometimes of cotton, and had a diameter of twenty-eight
feet. In the middle of it was circular hole (the vent) twenty-two
inches in diameter. This vent prevented undue strain on the canopy when it began to open and was said to reduce oscillation.
The rigging lines attaching the canopy to the harness (plates 39,
40) were twenty-two feet long. When not in use the parachute re-
posed in its bag, put there by an expert packer. (About twenty-
five minutes were needed to inspect and pack a parachute.) It
was not permitted to remain longer than two months in its bag
nor was it to be used for more than twenty-five descents. The
packers, who for the most part were women belonging to the
Women's Auxiliary Air Force, performed a highly skilled and
vital service.

The Parachute Smock
The parachute harness was worn over the zip-fronted gabardine
smock or 'jump jacket' (plates 42,44). In order to avoid the poss-
ibility of the paratrooper's equipment or weapons becoming en-
tangled in his parachute harness or being caught up on any pro-
jecting part of the aircraft's interior this smock was worn over all
other forms of dress and equipment (plate 43). It was normally
discarded by the wearer on landing.

The Denison Smock
Beneath the jump jacket the paratrooper wore either his battledress (plate 43) or, after its introduction for airborne service, the
Denison smock, a camouflage garment made from windproof
material with large pockets, over which he wore the web equipment normally carried into battle by every airborne soldier.
(plates 60-63). The Denison smock was a very practical garment
for use in the field. It was manufactured from heavy-duty windproof material and was camouflaged with a ragged pattern of
brown and darkish green printed over a lighter green base. (See
colour plates.) The smock was lined with a thick khaki-coloured
blanket lining, had large patch pockets closed with snap-press
studs and was zip-fastened right down the front. Hanging from
the lower edge at the rear of the smock was a 'tailpiece' — a flap
which was drawn up between the wearer's legs under the crotch,
and the end of which fastened in position on the front of the
smock to one of a series of three pairs of snap-press studs. (See
cover illustration — in a slightly modified form this garment is
still used by British airborne troops.)

Paratrooper's Battledress
Under the Denison smock the paratrooper wore his two-piece
khaki serge battledress consisting of a blouse and trousers buck-
ling at the wrists and ankles. The trousers worn by paratroopers
for operational use differed slightly from the normal issue battledress trousers in that they had, on the exterior of the left leg, a
large expanding map pocket (plates 18, 19).

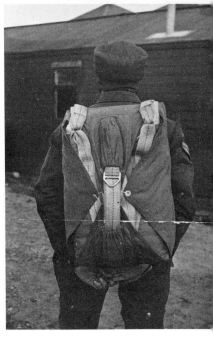

Above: *Six photographs taken
in October 1941, showing
British Airborne Special
clothing and equipment.*
42. Top left: *The gabardine
jump smock, closely modelled
on the German paratroop
smock.*
43. Top centre: *The jump
smock opened to show the
wearer's equipment worn under
the smock and over the
battledress.*

44. **Top right:** *A paratrooper helping to fix a colleague's parachute harness.*
45. **Below left:** *Detail of the parachute pack.*
46. **Below centre:** *Close-up of the early pattern crepe rubber soled ankle boots.*
47. **Below right:** *The cloth covered rubber training helmet. This is an early pattern of the standard issue training helmet.*

Paratroop Boots
Canvas web anklets were worn with the issue black leather boots. At first the boots used were provided with thick crepe rubber soles (plates 46), but this was later found unnecessary; thereafter ordinary leather-soled army ankle boots with metal studs were worn (plate 64).

The Parachute/Fighting Knife
The all-important parachute knife, very similar to the commando fighting knife, was issued to all paratroops. With this knife the parachutist could, if necessary, cut himself free from his parachute harness. It was normally carried strapped to his right leg. (plate 16).

48

49

50

51

52

53

Airborne Headdress

Headdress used by British paratroops was of three basic types. Initially the beret, the forage cap or the service dress cap were worn, but these were eventually replaced by the distinctive 'red beret'; this head-gear was proudly worn by all qualified paratroops (plate 59).

Training Headdress

Early attempts at providing the paratroop recruits with a shock-proof rubber helmet for wear during training and practice jumps were relatively crude (plate 49). However, these soon developed into the standard pattern cloth-covered rubber helmet which, after its introduction, continued in use as a training helmet for the rest of the war (plates 3,9,14,43,47,50,72).

The Airborne Forces' Steel Helmet

Steel helmets used by the airborne forces had to fulfil three basic needs. They had to provide the wearer with adequate protection against shrapnel or gunfire; to be designed in such a way as to resist hard blows that might possibly be encountered during landings from an air drop, and at the same time to be so shaped as to prevent any part of the helmet becoming fouled with rigging or harness lines. The steel helmets in use at various times by the air-

48: Early attempts to provide protective headdress resulted in close fitting leather helmets being issued to the paratroop volunteers.
49: Prototype training helmets were manufactured from slabs of thick 'sorbo' rubber shaped and bonded together to give protection to the wearer's head and neck.
50: The regulation pattern training helmet, developed from the prototype.
51: Early airborne steel helmets had the additional fixture of a hard rubber rim fitted to the edge of the helmet shell.
52: Camouflage netting worn over the airborne helmet.
53: The rimless steel helmet with a painted side 'flash'.

24

54

55

56

57

58

59

54: *A painted helmet flash.*
55: *Details of the neck and chin straps designed for use on the airborne helmet. The leather straps were eventually replaced by web straps. It was found that perspiration affected the leather and made the threading of the straps through the metal rings which fastened the straps very difficult.*
56: *Details of the chin cup.*
57: *War Correspondent Alan Wood wearing a late wartime pattern airborne steel helmet with a thinner rim.*
58: *Additional helmet camouflage was provided by a netting cover with strips of hessian scrim attached.*
59: *The distinctive maroon coloured 'red beret'.*

borne troops differed only very slightly in their appearance (plates 51-58). The final helmet form adoped was a very good example of the way in which an item of protective equipment developed and proven in use by the German paratroop arm was carefully studied, copied in a modified form, and eventually adopted for use by the British airborne forces. Apart from the helmet's similarity in overall shape, the system adopted by the British for the chin and neck straps (plates 55, 56, 57) closely resembled in appearance the German version (plate 4); however, on the British pattern a chin cup was added to the helmet straps designed to fit closely around the wearer's chin and the lower part of his jaw (plate 56). This helped to ensure that the helmet, when worn under air drop or battle conditions, would grip the head more securely than would be the case if the helmet had only a thin chin or neck strap.

Helmet Camouflage
Additional camouflage to the helmet was provided by the use of a darkish green string net worn over the helmet and held in position by having the edges of the net drawn together under the helmet rim (plates 55, 56). This netting was sometimes garnished with foliage or sacking strips to further disrupt the outline of the helmet (plate 58).

Web Equipment and Chest Respirators

With the exception of the chest respirator (the military version of the gas mask and carrying case) the basic web equipment used by British airborne troops was identical to that used by all other British troops who, during the Second World War, wore two patterns of web equipment — the Pattern 1937 and Pattern 1944. The British paratrooper tended to use the 1937 pattern equipment (plates 60-66) almost until the end of the war in Europe. A set of 1937 pattern web equipment as used for infantry comprised the following parts:

2¼in wide waistbelt
Pair of braces
Two basic pouches
Bayonet frog
A waterbottle carrier for the Mk. VII bottle
Haversack
Pair of shoulder straps for the haversack
Pack
Two supporting straps.

The Chest Respirator used by British paratroops (or rather the carrying case used with the Chest Respirator) differed from the normal respirator in one respect. Normally, the military respirator was carried in the 'alert' position — that is the gas mask and case worn on the wearer's chest, hung from his neck by the case-carrying strap and held in position against his body by a thin cord attached to both sides of the case and tied around his back. This position allowed the soldier, if threatened by a gas attack, to reach quickly for the gas mask and, taking the mask from the case, put it on over his face and head; the breathing apparatus and gas filters remained inside the case. However, the British paratrooper's method of wearing the respirator was slightly different. Until the chest respirator was replaced by the small version introduced later in the war (plates 62,63), it was carried on operational air drops upside down on the front of the chest (plates 14,72); the carrying-case was worn over the parachute harness hung around the neck and was held in position against the wearer's body by the use of two short lengths of canvas webbing stitched on to the sides of the gas mask carrying-case at the base. These two straps were looped around the parachute harness and the loose ends were then fastened with press studs on to the case (plate 14). Removing the gas mask from the case when worn in this position was very simple indeed: undoing the carrying-case flap allowed the gas mask to drop out of the case.

60-63. Above: *Equipment and clothing worn by airborne troops for ground combat consisted of the Denison smock worn over the battledress; the face veil worn over the shoulders or around the neck; web equipment which included the waist belt, basic pouches and supporting straps, the haversack, entrenching tool and haft with carrier, gas mask and canvas container, bayonet with frog, cloth ammunition bandolier, binoculars, and a toggle rope for general towing purposes. Ankle boots, canvas gaiters and steel helmet with netting cover completed the outfit.*

64, 65. Below left and centre: *Uniforms and equipment as worn by airborne troops acting as infantry.*

66. Below right: *Members of the US Army Air Force Troop Carrier Command converse with British paratroopers who are wearing the sleeveless jump smock introduced for the D-Day landings and worn over their Denison jackets, battledress and equipment. The smocks had a full length zip down the front to enable the wearer to remove the garment with speed.*

67. Top left: *A paratroop sergeant armed with a Sten gun.*

68. Top centre: *A young paratroop officer armed with a Webley service revolver, seen during a training exercise held in the Norwich area of Eastern Command, June 1941.*

69. Top right: *A photograph taken during a training drop in August 1942 at Ringway, showing a paratrooper manning a Bren machine-gun.*

70. Below left: *An airborne soldier carrying a Colt Browning automatic pistol. A Canadian-manufactured version of the Belgian GP35, the magazine held thirteen rounds, which made the pistol a favourite with airborne and special service forces.*

71. Below centre: *A paratroop corporal with a Lee-Enfield rifle. Badges of rank and paratroop 'wings' were normally worn on the right arm of the para smock.*

72. Below right: *A picture of 'true grit' and determination. A sergeant paratrooper poses with a Thompson submachine-gun.*

73

75

74

73, 74: *The lightweight coll-apsible trolley used by air-borne troops to haul supplies by a 3 or 5 man team.*
75: *The first pattern fold-ing bicycle for paratroops.*
76: *The second pattern fold-ing bicycle for paratroops.*
77: *Paratroops at a London station prior to their de-parture for Europe, June 1944. The method of stowing and carrying equipment and weap-ons on the second pattern folding bicycle can be seen.*
78: *The lightweight high speed 2-stroke engined motor cycle, especially designed for use by airborne forces.*
79: *The lightweight collap-sible motorcycle of 1942, popularly known as the Corgi but officially designated the Wellbike.*
80: *A paratrooper about to bring his Wellbike into act-ion just after dropping. These bikes proved invaluable when establishing inter-unit con-tact within the dropping zone.*

76

78

79

77

80

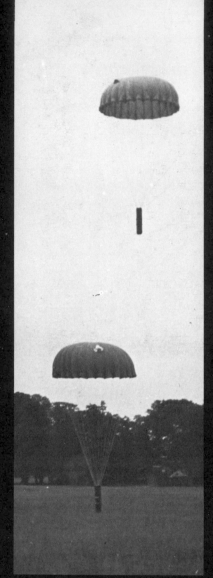

81: *Parachute containers descending during an airborne exercise.*

Right, top to bottom:

82: *The Wellbike miniature motorcycle, shown here packed into its container.*

83: *Every effort was made to supply newly landed airborne forces with essential supplies and equipment. Shown here is a Mark I container fully packed, with the lid open (left), packed and secured ready for use (centre) and, right, a selection of infantry weapons.*

84: *Making final adjustments to the fitting of a container slung below an aircraft.*